SandCastle 3

Vowel Blends

ee

Mary Elizabeth Salzmann

Published by SandCastle™, an imprint of ABDO Publishing Company, 4940 Viking Drive, Edina, Minnesota 55435.

Printed in the United States.

Cover and interior photo credits: Comstock, Corbis Images, Eyewire Images, PhotoDisc

Library of Congress Cataloging-in-Publication Data

Salzmann, Mary Elizabeth, 1968-
    Ee / Mary Elizabeth Salzmann.
        p. cm. -- (Vowel blends)
    ISBN 1-57765-455-2
    1. Readers (Primary) [1. English language--Phonetics.] I. Title.

PE1119 .S23422 2001
428.1--dc21

                                                                00-055852

The SandCastle concept, content, and reading method have been reviewed and approved by a national advisory board including literacy specialists, librarians, elementary school teachers, early childhood education professionals, and parents.

Let Us Know

After reading the book, SandCastle would like you to tell us your stories about reading. What is your favorite page? Was there something hard that you needed help with? Share the ups and downs of learning to read. We want to hear from you! To get posted on the ABDO Publishing Company Web site, send us email at:

sandcastle@abdopub.com

About SandCastle™

Nonfiction books for the beginning reader

- Basic concepts of phonics are incorporated with integrated language methods of reading instruction. Most words are short, and phrases, letter sounds, and word sounds are repeated.

- Readability is determined by the number of words in each sentence, the number of characters in each word, and word lists based on curriculum frameworks.

- Full-color photography reinforces word meanings and concepts.

- "Words I Can Read" list at the end of each book teaches basic elements of grammar, helps the reader recognize the words in the text, and builds vocabulary.

- Reading levels are indicated by the number of flags on the castle.

Look for more SandCastle books in these three reading levels:

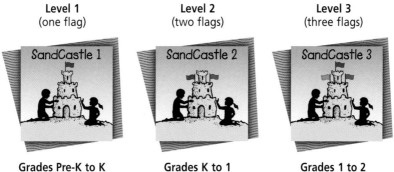

Level 1 (one flag)	Level 2 (two flags)	Level 3 (three flags)
Grades Pre-K to K	**Grades K to 1**	**Grades 1 to 2**
5 or fewer words per page	5 to 10 words per page	10 to 15 words per page

ee

Bree and Keenan have fun feeding the geese with their grandparents.

ee

Keene has a parakeet on his shoulder.

He named it Peep.

Breena leans against
a tree.

She blows on a dandelion
and the seeds fly away.

ee

Reece and his dad work on the wheel of his bike.

ee

Reese and Sandeep carry the basket of corn between them.

Mateen holds the wheel and helps his dad steer the tractor.

ee

Lee and his family walk down the street.

His sister has bare feet.

ee

Dee sits with her friend Sheena.

Dee has dimples in her cheeks.

Deena pretends to call her friend Kaylee.

What color is her phone?

(green)

Words I Can Read

Nouns

A noun is a person, place, or thing

basket (BASS-kit) p. 13
bike (BIKE) p. 11
cheeks (CHEEKSS) p. 19
color (KUHL-ur) p. 21
corn (KORN) p. 13
dad (DAD) pp. 11, 15
dandelion (DAN-duh-lye-uhn) p. 9
dimples (DIM-puhlz) p. 19

family (FAM-uh-lee) p. 17
feet (FEET) p. 17
friend (FREND) pp. 19, 21
fun (FUHN) p. 5
geese (GEESS) p. 5
grandparents (GRAND-pa-ruhntss) p. 5
green (GREEN) p. 21

parakeet (PA-ruh-keet) p. 7
phone (FOHN) p. 21
seeds (SEEDZ) p. 9
shoulder (SHOHL-dur) p. 7
sister (SISS-tur) p. 17
street (STREET) p. 17
tractor (TRAK-tur) p. 15
tree (TREE) p. 9
wheel (WEEL) pp. 11, 15

Proper Nouns

A proper noun is the name of a person, place, or thing

Bree (BREE) p. 5
Breena (BREE-nuh) p. 9
Dee (DEE) p. 19
Deena (DEE-nuh) p. 21
Kaylee (KAY-lee) p. 21
Keenan (KEEN-uhn) p. 5

Keene (KEEN) p. 7
Lee (LEE) p. 17
Mateen (ma-TEEN) p. 15
Peep (PEEP) p. 7
Reece (REESS) p. 11

Reese (REESS) p. 13
Sandeep (san-DEEP) p. 13
Sheena (SHEE-nuh) p. 19

22

Pronouns

A pronoun is a word that replaces a noun

he (HEE) p. 7   **she** (SHEE) p. 9   **what** (WUHT) p. 21
it (IT) p. 7   **them** (THEM) p. 13

Verbs

A verb is an action or being word

blows (BLOHZ) p. 9   **have** (HAV) p. 5   **pretends**
call (KAWL) p. 21   **helps** (HELPSS) p. 15   (pree-TENDZ) p.21
carry (KA-ree) p. 13   **holds** (HOHLDZ) p. 15   **sits** (SITSS) p. 19
feeding (FEED-ing) p. 5   **is** (IZ) p. 21   **steer** (STIHR) p. 15
fly (FLYE) p. 9   **leans** (LEENZ) p. 9   **walk** (WAWK) p. 17
has (HAZ) pp. 7, 17, 19   **named** (NAYMD) p. 7   **work** (WURK) p. 11

Adjectives

An adjective describes something

bare (BAIR) p. 17   **his** (HIZ) pp. 7, 11, 15, 17   **their** (THAIR) p. 5
her (HUR) pp. 19, 21

Adverbs

An adverb tells how, when, or where
something happens

away (uh-WAY) p. 9

23

Glossary

dandelion – A plant with bright yellow flowers that is often found on lawns.

parakeet – A small parrot with brightly colored feathers and a long, pointed tail.

tractor – A powerful vehicle with large tires used to pull farm machinery or other heavy loads.

More ee Words

bee	feel	see
beep	free	sheep
beetle	gee	sleep
creep	keep	sweet
deer	meet	three
eel	queen	week